I0144118

Copyright 2014 @ Roho Publishing. All rights reserved. Printed in the United States.

ISBN:978-0-9894338-4-6
Cover Design and Front Cover Photo: Jenna Stanbrough

Roho Publishing
4040 Graphic Arts Road
Emporia, KS 66801

www.rohopublishing.com

About Roho Publishing

When Kip Keino defeated Jim Ryun in the 1968 Olympic Games at 1500 meters he credited the win to "Roho." Roho is the Swahili word for spirit demonstrated through extraordinary strength and courage. The type of courage and strength that can be summoned up from deep within that will allow you to meet your goals and overcome the challenges in life. Roho Publishing focuses on the spirit of sport and is designed to inspire, encourage, motivate, and teach valuable life lessons.

Dedication

To all the passionate and positive leaders who work with young people on a daily basis to make a difference.

Acknowledgements

Thanks to my daughter Jenna for the cover design, page layout and editing.

Thanks to my daughters, Bethany and Leslie for their reviews of the manuscript.

To my wife, Wendy, my pot-of-gold at the end of the rainbow.

To my parents, my lifetime motivation.

Contents

10. Teamwork

Introduction

Stories have the ability to raise our spirits, to encourage and motivate us, and to teach us valuable life lessons. They can be used as stepping stones towards living a better life.

The sixty stories in *Developing Character Through Motivational Fables* are full of inspiration and motivation. Some are fables using stories of animals, plants, or forces of nature and others are parables illustrating a learning lesson. The stories demonstrate the qualities necessary to be successful in life: good character, integrity, a strong work ethic, dedication, and perseverance. Many of the stories have been passed down through history, but all of the stories have a lesson.

Storytelling has always been a powerful tool for learning. Stories can ignite listeners' imaginations through use of language and visual imagery. In many traditional tribes, it was an individual's skill as a storyteller that was a deciding factor in that person's being chosen as chief or respected elder for the tribe.

Stories are a powerful resource for communication and for delivering a memorable and inspiring message. Classic fables have been traditionally used to teach morals to both children and adults alike. Those morals are just as relevant today in the modern world as they were many years ago when they were first written.

Stories have had a powerful effect for thousands of years and they continue to be a part of our culture today, in terms of helping us acquire knowledge and enhance our learning and development. If the listener can identify with a story and draw a parallel between it and the action in their own life, they become much more focused on the plot, deriving some learning from the underlying message of it.

Whether read aloud, told to a group, or used for personal reading, stories can have a very powerful impact. Stories can take us back down memory lane to our childhood days, when we heard stories both at home and at school. Story time was a special time, even if you didn't like school!

In today's modern world, the purpose of stories continues to be to communicate information to hand down cultural values, to educate and to facilitate, to learn, and to grow and develop. Many stories conclude with a happy ending such as "they lived happily ever" leaving readers in a positive mood. These happy ending stories give enthusiasm, courage, hope, and optimism for the future.

The stories are designed to encourage reflective thinking. They all have in common an end purpose, which is to help the reader see a situation from a different point of view which offers an opportunity for learning. The meaning of the story can mean different things to different people. Be careful of forcing readers to accept only one interpretation of the meaning of the story. Different valid opinions add to the richness of discussion. The questions are designed to generate productive discussion around the story. They provide a start to get discussion going.

There are many ways the questions can be used. Here are ten suggestions.

1. Post on bulletin board for all to read.

2. Distribute event specific stories.

3. The leader reads the story and then a group discussion takes place.

4. Individuals are assigned to read stories to a group. Group discussion takes place after the story is read.

5. An individual reads the story within a small group. Small group discussion takes place after the story is read.

6. A group discusses questions during an activity.

7. Stories can be read during a break in activity.

8. Questions can be discussed during a break in activity.

9. Reading of the story and discussion on stories can take place at the end of an activity.

10. Individuals can be given a story to help motivate them under specific situations such as when injured, performance is sub-par, or a person is depressed.

The Butterfly

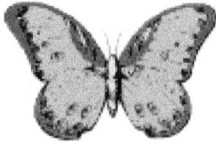

A man found a cocoon for a butterfly. One day a small opening appeared, he sat and watched the butterfly for several hours as it struggled to force its body through the little hole. Then it seemed to stop making any progress. It appeared as if it had gotten as far as it could and could go no farther. So the man decided to help the butterfly. He took a pair of scissors and snipped the remaining bit of the cocoon. The butterfly then emerged easily; however, something was strange. The butterfly's body was swollen and its wings were shriveled. The man continued to watch the butterfly because he expected at any moment, the wings would enlarge and expand to be able to support the body, which would contract in time. However, that did not happen.

The butterfly spent the rest of its life crawling around with a swollen body and deformed wings. It was never able to fly. What the man in his kindness and haste did not understand, was that the restricting cocoon and the struggle required for the butterfly to get through the small opening of the cocoon is the way to force fluid from the body of the butterfly into its wings so that it would be ready to fly.

Sometimes struggles are what we need in life. If we go through all our life without any obstacles, that would cripple us. We would not be as strong as what we could have been. It is the struggles we encounter in life that allow us to fly!

Affirmation: I accept challenges in order to get better.

To think about:

1. What struggles have you encountered and survived that have made you better?

2. What have you learned from your struggles?

3. Have you appreciated an accomplishment more after you had many barriers to overcome to achieve it?

The greater the challenge, the greater the reward. -Unknown

Buzzard, Bat, and Bumblebee

If a bumblebee is dropped into an open glass, it would be unable to get out and eventually die unless it is helped out. It will not see the way to escape at the top and will continually try to find some way out through the sides near the bottom. It will continue to seek a way where none exists, until it destroys itself and dies.

A bat is a remarkable animal as it flies through the night air. However it, cannot take off from a level place. When it is placed on flat ground, all it can do is shuffle about helplessly. It needs to reach some slight elevation from which it can throw itself into the air and then take off.

A buzzard placed in an eight foot square pen that is entirely open at the top is unable to escape. A buzzard has to begin a flight from the ground with a run of at least 10 feet. Without space to run, the buzzard will not even attempt to fly, staying a prisoner in a small jail without a top.

Many people are like the buzzard, the bat, and the bee. They struggle with their problems and frustrations, not realizing that there is an easy answer to the problem.

Affirmation: I put my plan to work!

To think about:

1. Have you had a problem that you thought was bigger than it actually was? How did you resolve the problem?

2. How important is it to set a goal and then a plan to achieve the goal? How helpful is a goal without a plan to achieve it?

3. Think of a goal you may have now. What are the steps you will need to achieve in order to successfully reach your goal?

A dream is just a dream. A goal is a dream with a plan and a deadline. -Harvey Mackay

Eagles in a Storm

An eagle knows when a storm is approaching long before it actually arrives. The eagle will fly to a high spot and wait for the winds to come. When the storm arrives, it sets its wings so that the wind will pick it up and lift it above the storm. The eagle does not escape the storm. The eagle uses the storm to lift it higher. The storm rages below while the eagle is soaring above it.

People face many storms in life. If we set our minds with positive thoughts, we can rise above them. Our attitude can lift us above the storms.

With the help of others, we can ride the winds of the storm that bring injury, sickness, tragedy, failure, and disappointment in our lives and soar above the storm.

It is not the burdens of life that weigh us down but how we handle them.

Affirmation: I stay positive at all times.

To think about:

1. Think about times when practice, competition, or life is hard. Do you let the storm of difficult times get you down?

2. How can you rise above the storm when life is tough?

3. How can you help others rise above the storm?

It is not the burdens of life that weigh us down, it is how we handle them. -Unknown

Get Up Giraffe

The interaction between a mother and baby giraffe immediately after birth is an amazing sight. The baby giraffe falls 10 feet from its mother's womb and usually lands on its back. Within seconds it rolls over and tucks its legs under its body. Then the mother giraffe rudely introduces its offspring to the reality of life.

The mother giraffe positions herself directly over her calf and then swings her long leg out and kicks her baby, and the baby giraffe is sent sprawling head over heels. When it doesn't get up, the mother giraffe repeatedly kicks the baby over and over again. The baby calf struggles to rise but cannot quite make it. As the baby calf grows tired, the mother kicks it again to stimulate its efforts. Finally, the calf stands for the first time on its wobbly legs.

Then the mother giraffe does the most remarkable thing. She kicks it off its feet again. Why? She wants it to remember how it got up. In the wild, baby giraffes must be able to get up as quickly as possible to stay with the herd, where there is safety. Lions, hyenas, and leopards all enjoy young giraffes. The young giraffe would be dinner, if the mother didn't teach her calf to get up quickly.

Like the giraffe, people have a vision or dream of something that should be accomplished and they go to work. They are often knocked down and, for years they may seemingly go nowhere. But every time successful people are knocked down they stand back up. You cannot destroy these people and at the end of their career, they've accomplished a significant goal.

Affirmation: I rise to the challenge.

To think about:

1. How quickly do you get up when you have been knocked down?

2. How do you grow from your failures?

3. Has someone, such as a boss, teacher, etc., challenged you to become better and you didn't understand the process at the time? How did you react to the challenge?

It's not whether you get knocked down; it's whether you get up. -Vince Lombardi

Our greatest glory is not in never failing, but in rising up every time we fail. -Ralph Waldo Emerson

How High Can You Jump?

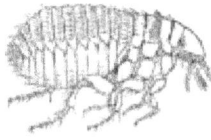

You train fleas by putting them in a jar with a top on it. Fleas like to jump, so they will jump up and hit the top over and over again. As you watch them jump and hit the top, you will notice something interesting. The fleas continue to jump, but they are no longer jumping high enough to hit the top.

If you take the top off, the fleas continue to jump, but they won't jump out of the jar. The reason is simple. They have conditioned themselves to jump a certain height. Once they have conditioned themselves to jump that height, that's all they can do.

Many times, people do the same thing. They restrict themselves and never reach their potential. Just like the fleas, they fail to jump higher, thinking they are doing all they can do.

Affirmation: I have the courage to move out of my comfort zone.

To think about:

1. What limits do you place on yourself?

2. How can you remove the limits that will keep you from reaching your potential?

3. How can other people help you go beyond your self-imposed limits?
   1. How can you help them?

Move out of your comfort zone. You can only grow if you are willing to feel awkward and uncomfortable when you try something new. -Brian Tracy

Mule In The Well

Stepping Up To Challenge- One Day At A Time

One day a farmer's mule (Warwick) fell down into a well. The animal cried for hours as the farmer tried to figure out what to do. Finally he decided the animal was old and the well needed to be covered up anyway, it just wasn't worth it to retrieve the mule. So he invited all his neighbors to come over and help him. They all grabbed a shovel and began to shovel dirt into the well.

At first, the mule realized what was happening and cried horribly. Then, to everyone's amazement, he quieted down. A few shovel loads later, the farmer finally looked down the well and was astonished at what he saw.

With every shovel of dirt that hit his back, the mule was doing something amazing. He would shake it off and take a step up. As the farmer's neighbors continued to shovel dirt on top of the animal, he would shake it off and take a step up. Pretty soon, everyone was amazed as the mule stepped up over the edge of the well and trotted off.

Life is going to shovel dirt on you. The trick to getting out of the well is to shake it off and take a step up. Each of our troubles is a stepping stone. We can get out of the deepest wells just by not giving up! Shake it off and take a step up!

Life can be difficult; but if you are tough, you will improve one day at a time. Take a step up every day to get better.

Affirmation: I get better every day.

To think about:

1. What are the little things you can do to improve one day at a time?

2. How will you handle fatigue and frustration when you want to give up?

3. What is the mental attitude you need to step up and be successful?

There is no one giant step that does it. It's a lot of little steps. -Peter Cohen

Rock

An old farmer had plowed around a large rock in one of his fields for years. He had broken several plowshares and had grown quite frustrated working around the rock. After breaking another plowshare one day, and remembering all the trouble the rock had caused him through the years, he finally decided to do something about it. When he put the crowbar under the rock, he was surprised to discover that it was only about six inches thick and that he could break it up easily with a sledgehammer. As he was carting the pieces away he had to smile, remembering all the trouble that the rock had caused him over the years and how easy it would have been to get rid of it sooner.

Affirmation: I tackle challenges head-on.

To think about:

1. Have you had "a rock" in your life that you have procrastinated moving? How did you finally break up "the rock?"

2. Recognize "a rock" in your life now. What can you do to break it up?

3. How does it feel to successfully remove "a rock" in your way?

Obstacles don't have to stop you. If you run into a wall, don't turn around and give up. Figure out how to climb it, go through it, or work around it. -Michael Jordan

Sisu

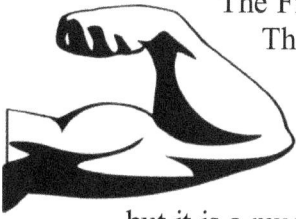

The Finns have something they call "sisu," which dates back hundreds of years. The word defines the entire country of Finland and is loosely translated into English as strength of will, determination, perseverance, and acting in the face of adversity. It is a mixture of bravery, of ferocity and tenacity, of the ability to keep fighting after most people would have quit, and to fight with the will to win. The Finns translate sisu as "the Finnish spirit," but it is a much more gutful word than that.

The word is widely considered to lack a proper translation into any other language. "Having guts" is the English-to-Finnish formal translation, as the word derives from sisus, which means something inner or interior.

Sisu is about taking action against the odds and displaying courage and resoluteness in the face of adversity. Deciding on a course of action and then sticking to that decision against repeated failures is sisu. Sisu means going beyond one´s mental or physical capacity. It is about being bold enough to cover unknown terrain, to see beyond one's perceived capacities and to take risks, all while being flexible and tolerating uncertainty. It is about bending but not breaking. Sisu begins where your perseverance ends.

Although, sisu is a Finnish term, it is a universal quality which everyone shares. Any event can be seen either as an opportunity or an obstacle, and the person's attitude greatly influences the actions taken as a result. Developing and cultivating sisu is about awakening potential and igniting hope. It is about seeing what we might be, pushing beyond what we perceive our abilities to be, and forcing ourselves through the pain barrier.

The age-old concept of sisu can empower us to turn challenges into opportunities, to turn barriers into accomplishments. Using sisu, we can build a bridge toward our current self and our best future self.

Affirmation: Sisu=guts.

To think about:

1. How can the concept of "sisu" help you to become better?

2. On a scale of 1-10 (1 low, 10 high), rate your level of sisu.

3. Does sisu arise from within (an internal influence) or from without (an external influence)?

Persistence is probably the single most common quality of high achievers. They simply refuse to give up. They longer you hang in there, the greater the chance that something will happen in your favor. No matter how hard it seems, the longer you persist the more likely your success. -Jack Canfield

Elephants Beeware

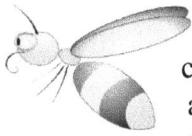

A bee's stinger cannot penetrate most areas of an elephant's tough hide, but it can penetrate around the eyes where the skin is much thinner and on the inside of an elephant's sensitive trunk. Stings in these areas are very painful and the elephant remembers this experience.

Research shows elephants make a rumbling sound or alarm call to warn their fellow herd members of imminent danger when bees are discovered. When this rumbling sound is recorded and played to other groups of elephants, it causes them to respond with similar alarm. Even a recording of buzzing bees elicits the elephants alarm call.

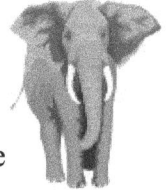

Some farmers in Africa have begun using "beehive" fences" to keep elephants out of areas where crops are growing. These fences are composed of beehives strung on wires. When elephants try to push through the wires, it shakes the hives and bees swarm out and sting the elephants. The elephants quickly learn to avoid the areas protected by the fences. Farmers like these fences because the hives also produce honey and which can be harvested and sold.

Affirmation: I do the small things to be successful.

To think about:

1. What should you focus on when the odds are stacked against you?

2. Small things can be important. List several things you do that may be considered small, yet they add up into success.

3. Think of a time you were the underdog, but believed in your abilities and were successful.

One person can make a difference and every person should try. -John F. Kennedy

California Gold Rush

There's a California gold rush story that tells of two brothers who sold all they had and went prospecting for gold. They discovered a vein of the shining ore, staked a claim, and proceeded to get down to the serious business of getting the gold out of the mine.

All went well at first, but then a strange thing happened. The vein of gold disappeared! They had come to the end of the rainbow, and the pot of gold was no longer there. The brothers continued to pick away, but without success. Finally, they gave up in disgust.

They sold their equipment and claim rights for a few hundred dollars, and took the train back home. Now the man who bought the claim hired an engineer to examine the rock strata of the mine. The engineer advised him to continue digging in the same spot where the former owners had left off. And three feet deeper, the new owner struck gold.

A little more persistence and the two brothers would have been millionaires themselves. There is gold in you, too. If you are willing to dig for it!

Affirmation: I dig deep within myself.

To think about:

1. Do you give up before you achieve success?

2. If you dig a little deeper what will you find?

3. List three specific things that you could do to dig a little deeper.

We found out he will fight when it comes down to the finish. Today he had to dig down a little and he showed he has some guts. -Bill Mott

The Power of a Penny Doubled

One day, a rich merchant said to his young son, "Son, I have an important question to ask you. I will give you the total amount of one penny doubled each day for one month or a million dollars cash right now. Which will you choose?" The son answered without hesitation, "The million dollars of course father."

Faced with the same question, which would you choose? The million dollars cash or the total amount of a single penny doubled each day for 30 days?

The wise father looks at the boy and with a knowing smile takes out paper and pen. "Son," he said quietly, "Come sit next to me and learn."

Let's study the power of a penny doubled. Follow how the money accumulates if that one shinny penny is doubled each day for 30 days in a lesson about wealth and patience. Believe it or not, you will end up with much more than a million dollars. The power of a single penny doubled is amazing isn't it?

The next time you see a penny on the street, make time to bend down and pick it up.

Affirmation: Hard work pays off.

To think about:

1. Do you have the patience to stick to your plan and gradually build yourself?

2. Think of a time where you struggled to get things going and eventually you reached a point where it just took off.

3. Starting with a penny is not much, but you have to start somewhere. What are the first steps in getting started towards your goals?

True progress quietly and persistently moves along without notice. -St. Francis of Assisi

Day 1: $.01	**Day 11:** $10.24	**Day 21:** $10,485.76
Day 2: $.02	**Day 12:** $20.48	**Day 22:** $20,971.52
Day 3: $.04	**Day 13:** $40.96	**Day 23:** $41,943.04
Day 4: $.08	**Day 14:** $81.92	**Day 24:** $83,886.08
Day 5: $.16	**Day 15:** $163.84	**Day 25:** $167,772.16
Day 6: $.32	**Day 16:** $327.68	**Day 26:** $335,544.32
Day 7: $.64	**Day 17:** $655.36	**Day 27:** $671,088.64
Day 8: $1.28	**Day 18:** $1,310.72	**Day 28:** $1,342,177.28
Day 9: $2.56	**Day 19:** $2,621.44	**Day 29:** $2,684,354.56
Day 10: $5.12	**Day 20:** $5,242.88	**Day 30:** $5,368,709.12

Two Frogs in the Milk

There once were two frogs. One was fat and the other was skinny. One day, while searching for food, they fell into a container of milk. The container was deep and the sides were slippery and try as hard as they could; they couldn't get out. All they could do was swim.

The fat frog said to the skinny frog, "There's no use swimming any longer. We're just going to drown, so we might as well give up." The skinny frog replied, "Keep paddling. Somebody will come along to help us." So they continued paddling for hours.

The fat frog was becoming very tired and said, "I'm becoming very tired now. I'm just going to stop paddling and drown. We're doomed. There's no possible way out of here." But the skinny frog said, "Keep trying. Keep paddling. Something will happen, keep paddling."

After two more hours the fat frog said, "I can't go on any longer. There's no sense in doing it because we're going to drown anyway. What's the use?" The fat frog stopped and gave up, falling to the bottom of the container and drowning in the milk. But the skinny frog kept on paddling.

Ten minutes later, the skinny frog felt something solid beneath his feet. His continual swimming had churned the milk into butter and he easily hopped out of the container.

Affirmation: Give up is not in my vocabulary.

To think about:

1. Do you wait for someone to come help you or do you make your own destiny?

2. Patience is often rewarded. On a scale of 1-10 how would you rate your patience?

3. What positive self-talk would be important when you feel like giving up?

You just can't beat the person who won't give up. -Babe Ruth

Are You Building a Cathedral?

A fable is told of three bricklayers who were all working on the same wall. Someone came up to the first man laying bricks and asked, "Sir, may I ask what you are doing?"

"I am laying bricks," he snapped sarcastically. "What does it look like I am doing?" And the man asked why are you doing that?" to which the first bricklayer replied, "It's to feed my family. I get $2 per brick," as he added mortar and placed another brick on the wall.

The man approached the second bricklayer and asked, "What are you doing?"

"I am building a wall. That's what I am doing." My workmates and I are great wall-builders and we enjoy building walls. We earn $2 per brick, which is pretty good pay around here."

Finally, the man approached the last bricklayer, finding him hard at work briskly laying bricks with exceptional excellence and speed. "What is it that you are doing?" the man asked in admiration. The third bricklayer said, "Why, I am part of a team that builds the best cathedrals in the land. My workmates and I build the walls for those cathedrals. The walls are probably the most important part of the cathedral, as they hold up what is a quite complex structure." The third bricklayer continued and pushed out his chest and said, "I am proud to be working for one of the single best builder of cathedrals in the country and I enjoy coming to work each day, being with my workmates and working with the other construction workers.

Affirmation: I take great pride in my work.

To think about:

1. Which bricklayer would you want working for you or would you want to work with?

2. What is your vision? Does it see the big picture?

3. Do you have an inspiring long term direction and purpose that keeps you motivated? If not, how could you go about creating that vision?

When love and skill work together, expect a masterpiece. -John Ruskin

Sand and Stone

Two friends were walking through the desert. During some point of the journey, they had an argument and one friend slapped the other one in the face. The one who got slapped was hurt, but without saying anything, wrote in the sand, *"Today my best friend slapped me in the face.'"*

They kept on walking until they found an oasis, where they decided to take a bath. The one who had been slapped got stuck in the mire and started drowning, but the friend saved him. After he recovered from the near drowning, he wrote on a stone, *'Today my best friend saved my life."*

The friend who had slapped and saved his best friend asked him, "After I hurt you, you wrote in the sand and now, you write on a stone, why?"

The friend replied, "When someone hurts us we should write it down in sand, where winds of forgiveness can erase it away. But, when someone does something good for us, we must engrave it in stone where no wind can ever erase it."

Learn to write your hurts in the sand and to carve your benefits in stone.

They say it takes a minute to find a special person, an hour to appreciate them, a day to love them, but then an entire life to forget them.

Do not value the things you have in your life, but value who you have in your life!

Affirmation: I help others reach their goals.

To think about:

1. Do you forgive people that have hurt you?

2. When someone does something good for you, how do you react?

3. When you do something good for someone, how does it feel?

**You will get all you want in life if you help enough other people get what they want.
-Zig Ziglar**

Two Ounces of Power

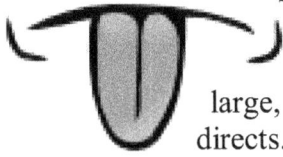

Some of the largest ships in the world weigh over 3 million tons and are the length of 15 football fields. They travel thousands of mile across the sea and often encounter fierce winds and high waves. Although the ship is large, they are guided by a very small rudder, wherever the will of the pilot directs.

Forest fires always start with one single spark either naturally caused by lightning or caused by humans. Either way, it takes just a single spark to ignite a large fire.

The average human tongue weighs only two ounces, but it is considered one of the strongest muscles in the body. Although the tongue weighs practically nothing, it is an amazing part of our body and is very powerful. Like the heart, the tongue is always working—helping mix food, forming letters and sounds, filtering out germs. Even while we sleep it constantly pushes saliva down our throats. It never rests!

The average person will say about 16,000 words per day. In one year, your words would fill 132 books with 400 pages in each. Roughly 20 percent of your life, you will spend talking! If there is negative thinking, the tongue will bring negative words. Foul speech, sloppy language, and hurtful words can come from a tongue guided by negative thoughts. But, conversely, if there are positive thoughts great things can happen.

The tongue can be compared to fire, but not water. A small glass of water wouldn't likely start a flood, but one small spark can destroy thousands of acres. The tongue has the same potential. We've heard the saying, "What's wrong? Cat got your tongue?" Well, maybe we should ask. "What's wrong? Negative thinking got your tongue?" Accentuate the positive in your words. Although it sounds simple, it yields powerful results. Accentuate the positive at every practice. It should be an essential characteristic of you and your team. Your words can be negative or positive.

Affirmation: I accentuate the positive.

To think about:

1. Why is it so hard to control the tongue?

2. Do you think the tongue is attached to the brain? If so how can you control it?

3. What is one tangible way that you can remind yourself today and every day about the power and purpose of your words?

Let your tongue speak what your positive mind thinks. **-Unknown**

The Problem May Be With Us

A man feared his wife wasn't hearing as well as she used to and he thought she might need a hearing aid. Not quite sure how to approach her, he called the family doctor to discuss the problem.

The doctor told him there is a simple informal test the husband could perform to give the doctor a better idea about her hearing loss. Here's what you do," said the doctor, "stand about 40 feet away from her, and in a normal conversational speaking tone see if she hears you. If not, go to 30 feet, then 20 feet, and so on until you get a response."

That evening, the wife is in the kitchen cooking dinner, and he was in the den. He says to himself, "I'm about 40 feet away, let's see what happens." Then in a normal tone he asks, 'Honey, what's for dinner?" No response.

So the husband moves to closer to the kitchen, about 30 feet from his wife and repeats, "Honey, what's for dinner?" Still no response

Next he moves into the dining room where he is about 20 feet from his wife and asks, Honey, what's for dinner?" Again he gets no response.

So he walks up to the kitchen door, about 10 feet away. "Honey, what's for dinner?"
Again there is no response.

So he walks right up behind her. "Honey, what's for dinner?" "James, for the **FIFTH** time I've said, **CHICKEN!"**

The problem may not be with the other person as we might think, but it could be with us!

Affirmation: I am a responsible person.

To think about:

1. How often do you blame somebody else to shift the blame from you?

2. Think of a time you didn't think it was your fault, but in reality it was.

3. How willing are you to step up and take responsibility?

Rather than looking for who to blame, look for the solution! -Catherine Pulsifer

A Leap of Encouragement

One day a group of frogs were hopping through the forest having a merry time when suddenly two frogs fell into a deep hole. The rest of the frogs quickly gathered around the hole to see what they could do to help their friends. When the frogs saw how deep the hole was, they all agreed that it was hopeless. With great sorrow they told the two frogs in the hole that they were as good as dead.

The two frogs in the hole weren't willing to give up and gathered up all their energy and began to jump as forcefully as they could. Their friends shouted into the hole that it was hopeless and they should have been more careful in the first place. They sorrowfully encouraged their friends in the hole that they should save their energy and give up as the situation was hopeless.

The two frogs continued jumping with all their might. They were both growing quite wearily after several unsuccessful hours of trying. Finally, one of the frogs finally started to believe his friends from above telling him it was hopeless. Exhausted, he gave up, lay down in the bottom of the hole, and quickly died.

The other frog was exhausted with pain pounding throughout his body, but he continued jumping as hard as he could. His friends above thought he was crazy and continued yelling for him to accept his fate and just die. But the determined frog just kept jumping harder and harder and amazingly he jumped so high that he jumped out of the hole.

Amazed, the other frogs cheered and gathered around him to ask "Why did you continue jumping when we told you it was impossible?"

The weary frog explained to them that he was deaf, and as he saw their gestures and shouting, he thought they were cheering him on. What he had perceived as encouragement inspired him to try harder and to succeed against all odds.

Affirmation: My words to others can make a positive difference.

To think about:

1. How can destructive words have an impact on the way others respond?

2. How can your encouraging words lift someone up and help them?

3. What words of kindness and encouragement can you speak to others?

If you fall behind, run faster. Never give up, never surrender, and rise up against the odds.
-Jesse Jackson

The Power of Encouragement

Dante Gabriel Rossetti, the famous 19th-century poet and artist, was once approached by an elderly man. The old fellow had some sketches and drawings that he wanted Rossetti to look at and tell him if they were any good, or if they at least showed potential talent.

Rossetti looked over them carefully. After the first few, he knew that they were worthless but Rossetti was a kind man, he told the elderly man as gently as possible that the pictures were without much value and showed little talent. He was sorry, but he could not lie to the man. The man was disappointed, but seemed to expect Rossetti's judgment. The old man then apologized for taking up Rossetti's time, but asked him to look at a few more drawings. Rossetti looked over the second batch of sketches and immediately became enthusiastic over the talent they revealed. "These," he said, "oh, these are good."

"This young student has a great talent. He should be given every help and encouragement. He has a great future." Rossetti could see that the old fellow was deeply moved. "Who is this fine young artist?" he asked. "Your son?"

"No," said the old man sadly. "It is me - 40 years ago. If only I had heard your praise then! For you see, I got discouraged and gave up – too soon."

Affirmation: By encouraging others, I help people achieve their goals.

To think about:

1. Who have you encouraged today?

2. How has someone made a difference in your life by encouraging you?

3. Think about how you can encourage people and help them to achieve their goals.

Kind words can be short and easy to speak, but their echoes are truly endless. -Mother Teresa

The Blind Men and the Elephant

Six blind men were discussing exactly what they believed an elephant to be, since each had heard how strange the creature was, yet none had ever seen one before. So the blind men agreed to find an elephant and discover what the animal was really like.

It didn't take the blind men long to find an elephant at a nearby market. The first blind man approached the beast and felt the animal's firm flat side. "It seems to me that the elephant is just like a wall," he said to his friends.

The second blind man reached out and touched one of the elephant's tusks. "No, this is round and smooth and sharp - the elephant is like a spear."

The third blind man stepped up to the elephant and touched its trunk. "Well, I can't agree with either of you; I feel a squirming writhing thing - surely the elephant is just like a snake."

The fourth blind man was of course by now quite puzzled. So he reached out, and felt the elephant's leg. "You are all talking complete nonsense," he said, "because clearly the elephant is just like a tree."

Utterly confused, the fifth blind man stepped forward and grabbed one of the elephant's ears. "You must all be mad - an elephant is exactly like a fan."

The sixth man approached, and, holding the beast's tail, disagreed again. "It's nothing like any of your descriptions - the elephant is just like a rope."

All six blind men continued to argue, based on their own particular experiences, as to what they thought an elephant was like. It was an argument that they were never able to resolve. Each of them was concerned only with their own idea. None of them had the full picture, and none could see any of the other's point of view.

There is never just one way to look at something - there are always different perspectives, meanings, and perceptions, depending on who is looking.

Affirmation: I try to understand other's viewpoints.

To think about:

1. How often are you tied to your point of view and unwilling to listen to others?

2. Do you agree with the phrase that you learn something from everyone you meet?

3. What does it take to see the full picture?

Every person you meet knows something you don't, learn from them. -H. Jackson Brown

Diamond in the Rough

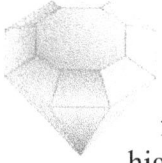

A diamond is one of the most precious stones in the world. It is highly valued and expensive in its final form. But a diamond starts out as a chunk of coal and is transformed by thousands of years of volcanic action that occurs during the formation of the earth's crust. Most natural diamonds are formed at high pressure, high-temperature conditions at depths of 87 to 120 miles below the earth's surface with the growth taking from 1 billion to 3.3 billion years. Diamonds are brought close to the Earth surface through deep volcanic eruptions by a magma, which cools into igneous rocks known as kimberlites. Inside the kimberlite are intermittent deposits of diamonds, one of several minerals present. It is from the tremendous pressure caused by the shifting nature of the earth's crust that forms diamonds. Under this pressure and time, the coal is transformed into a rough diamond, the hardest natural substance known in the world.

The character that we develop in life is a lot like the diamonds formed under pressure. Our character is formed under the pressures and challenges that we encounter on our long journey to success. The person that we become depends on how we respond to the pressures. Will we remain a chunk of coal or be patient and accept the challenges to become a shining diamond? Once a diamond is mined it must be cut and polished to establish its value. Like the diamond, we can establish value by polishing our skills on a continual basis. Our values increase as we stand up to the pressures of life and polish our skills for success.

Affirmation: My patience helps me to achieve success.

To think about:

1. Diamonds take billions of years to make. Think of a long range goal of yours that may take you many years to achieve.

2. How has or how will pressure made you a better person?

3. How will you continue to polish your skills on a continual basis?

A diamond is a chunk of coal that made good under pressure. -Henry Kissinger

Pain

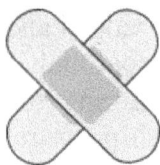

Do you think your physical training program designed by your coaches was meant to kill you? Maybe it was the warm-up that challenged your core. Maybe it was the running. Maybe it was a torturous drill that made the workout hard. How about the last few intervals of a hard workout? Coming around the last turn, your legs burned like they were on fire and it felt like someone stabbed you in the side with a knife. You were certain the coach's goal was to kill the team!

But the coaches weren't interested in how much you hurt that day. They were looking ahead to the season and were not only getting you ready for your first competition, but your last competition as well. Throughout the season, as your body became better conditioned, those drills and runs weren't as painful. They were still difficult, but they weren't as painful. The everyday pain made you better prepared for the season ahead.

Life is great; however, there is no promise that you will have a pain free life. In reality, mental and emotional pain is a part of the growing process. You may watch a parent, grandparent or child die. A relationship comes to an end. We lose when we expected to win. We fail a test. All of these are painful, but that pain doesn't necessarily equal harm. It equals growth and conditioning.

Today's pain may be preparing you for tomorrow. Look down the road to where you will be days, weeks, and even years from now. The coaches wanted you to be ready not just for today or tomorrow, but also for the rest of your lives. You just have to keep in mind that even though conditioning can be painful, it is a process to improve.

Affirmation: I fight through the pain.

To think about:

1. What pain do you have in your life?

2. Can you see how you can use pain to make you stronger or better prepared for tomorrow?

3. Do you know someone in pain today whom you could encourage? (Perhaps cheering your teammates on during a hard practice).

We must all suffer one of two things: the pain of discipline of the pain of regret or disappointment. -Jim Rohn

Relishing the Hard Button

HARD

You've seen the popular "easy" button. Just hit the easy button and things become easy. People love it. However, we know there are no easy buttons and no shortcuts to success. Successful people use the hard button. The hard button gives you a challenge. The hard button allows you to dig down, to make an unwavering commitment and dedication toward your goals. Winners resist the temptation to hit the easy button.

The easy button is a bright red shiny button. The hard button has a dull, well-used finish. It is chipped and worn because it has been around a long, long time.

Hitting the hard button reminds you to work harder. It reminds you to persevere. It gives you confidence that you are doing the right thing when others may be hitting the easy button. It tells you not to stop; you have to finish what you began. If you need to, you can hit the hard button again and again, as it never wears out. Using the hard button gives a tremendous amount of satisfaction and self-accomplishment.

Affirmation: I hit the hard button and relish the challenge.

To think about:

1. If you had the choice between the easy and the hard button, which would you choose? Why?

2. Describe the satisfaction you receive from a positive accomplishment.

3. Do you believe the quote, "The harder the challenge, the greater the reward?" Can you think of times when it has come true for you?

I learned the value of hard work by working hard. -Margaret Mead

Opportunity

In the days before modern harbors, a ship had to wait for the flood tide before it could make it to port. The Latin term for this situation of a ship in port waiting for the moment when it can ride the tide to harbor is "ob portu." The English word opportunity is derived from this original meaning. The captain and crew waited until the moment of high tide and had to be ready. They couldn't miss it. If they did, they would have to wait for another tide to come in. Shakespeare talked about the opportunity in the following passage.

There is a tide in the affairs of men,
Which, taken at the flood, leads on to fortune:
Omitted, all the voyage of their life
Is bound in shallows and in miseries.
On such a full sea are we now afloat;
And we must take the current when it serves,
Or lose our ventures.

Affirmation: I am ready when my opportunity comes.

To think about:

1. Do you waste precious opportunities or do you make the most of your opportunities?

2. Are you prepared when opportunity knocks?

3. How will you act fast and decisively the next time an opportunity comes?

Be ready when opportunity comes...Luck is the time when preparation and opportunity meet.
–Roy D. Chapin Jr.

Big Rocks

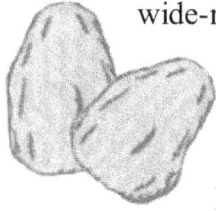

A teacher stood in front of a class and said, "Okay, time for a quiz." He pulled out a one-gallon, wide-mouthed Mason jar and set it on a table in front of him. Next, he produced about a dozen fist-sized rocks and carefully placed them, one at a time, into the jar. When the jar was filled to the top, and no more rocks would fit inside, he asked, "Is this jar full?" Everyone in the class said, "Yes."

He reached under the table and pulled out a bucket of gravel. He dumped some gravel in and shook the jar causing pieces of gravel to work themselves down into the spaces between the big rocks. Then he asked the group once more, "Is the jar full?" By this time the class was onto him. "Probably not," one of them answered. "Good," he replied. He reached under the table and brought out a bucket of sand. He started dumping the sand in, and it went into all the spaces left between the rocks and the gravel. Once more he asked the question, "Is this jar full?" "No," the class shouted. Once again he said, "Good." Then he grabbed a pitcher of water and began to pour it in until the jar was filled to the brim.

He looked up at the class and asked, "What is the point of this illustration?" One eager student raised his hand and said, "You can always do more."

"No," the speaker replied, "that's not the point. The point is, if you don't put the big rocks in first, you'll never get them in at all."

The big rocks are the things you value most in life. Put priority on them and take care of them first. Don't wait and think the big rocks will fall in place by themselves. There will always be space available in your life for the gravel, sand and water, but make space to place your big rocks in first.

Affirmation: I focus on my big rocks.

To think about:

1. What are the "big rocks" in your life? List at least four big rocks.

2. Are you too busy with the gravel, sand and water in your life to focus on what is really important?

3. How do you place the big rocks in your life first?

Decide what your priorities are and how much time you'll spend on them. If you don't, someone else will. -Harvey Mackay

How Do You Use Your Time?

Imagine there is a bank which credits your account each morning with $86,400. It carries over no balance from day to day, and every evening when you lie down to sleep, it eliminates whatever part of that amount you had failed to use during the day. And the only variable is that you don't know when your bank will stop this process. So, what would you do? You would find a way to spend it, right?

In theory, we all have such a bank. It's called "time." Every morning, you are credited with 86,400 seconds. Every night you have to write off as a loss whatever you failed to invest toward a good purpose. This account will not carry a balance over, either.

Remember that nothing is certain in this life. Each day is a new account opened for you. If you fail to use the day's deposits, the loss is yours. There is no going back; you must live on today's deposit.

Time is a wonderful gift! We need to take advantage of every second we have in all aspects of our lives. We may be on top at any given moment, but if we do not use the time we have to prepare for the next challenge, we may find ourselves behind.

Today, take the time to invest in yourself and others.

Affirmation: I use my time wisely.

To think about:

1. How do you spend your time? Do you focus on using every minute?

2. Do you take time to invest in others and in your relationships?

3. How could you spend your time more wisely?

It's not the years in your life that count. It's the life in your years. -Abraham Lincoln

One Thousand Marbles

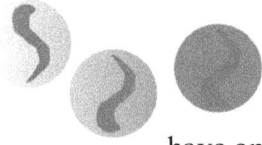

The average person lives about 75 years, some more and some less. Multiply 75 years by 52 weeks per year and you get 3,900, which is the number of weeks that the average person has in their lifetime. If you are age 15, you have an average of 3,120 weeks left. A 20 year old would have an average of 2,860 weeks left.

When John was 55 years old, he went to the store and bought 1,000 marbles to represent the average number of weeks he had left to live. Every Saturday, he threw away one marble. As John watched the marbles diminish, he started to focus more on the really important things in life. As his time on earth was running out, he began to get his priorities straight. At age 75, Tom took out the last marble and threw it away, counting his blessings that he had been given more time to achieve his goals on earth.

Affirmation: I live each day to the fullest.

To think about:

1. Do you have any days you feel are wasted? How will you make good use of the marbles you have left?

2. What are your priorities? Do you have a good perspective on your priorities?

3. Do you have timelines on your goals?

Carpe diem—Seize the day! -Unknown

Run Toward the Roar

When male lions get old, their teeth start to get rotten and they aren't able to kill animals very easily. In order to get food, they recruit the female lions and stronger young males to help them. When the lions get ready to hunt, the females and young lions go hide on one side of a herd while the big, old lion goes to the other side of it. Once he's in position, he'll let out a massive, scary roar that sends the herd running away from him, where the stronger lions are waiting. As the herd runs away from the roar they run to their death.

In life, you must do many things correctly, such as getting plenty of rest and exercise, eat right, and staying mentally strong. There are many things that we do not want to do because they are challenging and difficult. People often tend to procrastinate with high levels of anxiety on these difficult challenges.

The task we shy away from is like the old, roaring lion that has bad teeth and a big roar. Instead of running from the task, face the roar and run in the direction of what you fear, to accomplish the task.

When we dig into challenging work with a positive attitude and believe in ourselves, we realize, "this is not so bad after all." Take the challenge to "run toward the roar" and face your responsibilities head on. After all, the problem may only be an old, tooth decayed lion.

Affirmation: I step up to meet my challenges head on.

To think about:

1. What scares you?

2. What do you need to do in order to be able to "run toward the roar" today?

3. What tools do you have to help you as you "run toward the roar?"

Accept challenges, so that you may feel the exhilaration of victory. -George Patton

The Cafeteria of Life

An immigrant came to America from Europe. After he landed in New York City, his paperwork was processed and he felt hungry. He found a cafeteria and went inside to eat. He sat down at an empty table and waited for someone to take his order. Five minutes passed and still no one came to take his order. Ten minutes passed and then 15 minutes, and still no one had come to take his order. Finally, he saw a woman with a tray full of food sit down opposite him. He asked how she had gotten the food. "Start out at that end," she said. "Just go along the line and pick out what you want. At the other end they'll tell you how much you have to pay." The immigrant had never been to a cafeteria and did not know how it worked.

The cafeteria of life is open every day. If you are willing to pay the price with effort, work, and determination, you can get about anything you want. Success is available at the cafeteria of life, but it is not available if you wait for someone to bring it to you. You have to get up and go get it yourself.

Affirmation: I make wise choices and pursue them with a passion.

To think about:

1. Have you ever waited for something to happen and it never did until you started working harder at it?

2. What is available on the cafeteria of life for you? Do you know what you want?

3. You can't eat everything on the buffet. What choices in life will you pursue?

In life, many things will catch your eye, but only a few will catch your heart. Pursue those!"
-Unknown

Which Direction Do I Go?

The Cheshire Cat is a fictional cat popularized by Lewis Carroll in Alice's Adventures in Wonderland. The Cheshire Cat is the cat of the Duchess. Alice meets it when she leaves the Duchess' house, and finds it in a tree. It constantly grins and can disappear and reappear whenever it likes. Sometimes it disappears and leaves its grin behind.

The Cheshire Cat is the only character in Wonderland who actually listens to Alice. With his remarks, he teaches Alice the 'rules' of Wonderland. He gives her insight in how things work. One of the most famous Cheshire Cat quotes follows:

"Would you please tell me which way I ought to go?", said Alice.
"That depends on where you want to get to," said the Cheshire Cat
"I don't much care where," said Alice
"Then it doesn't matter which way you go," said the Cat
"So long as I get somewhere," said Alice
"Oh you're sure to do that," said the Cat, "If you only keep walking"
(quote from Alice's Adventures in Wonderland by Lewis Carroll)

Sometimes we simply act without focus and without really knowing where we'll end up. We tend to get caught up in things that don't really matter. We have been told numerous times that working hard is the key to success, but what's the point of hard work without knowing where you're going?

Affirmation: My commitment to my goals keeps me headed in the right direction.

To think about:

1. Do you know where you want to go or do you wander aimlessly without direction?

2. How do you figure out where you want to go?

3. How can a focus on goals send you in the right direction?

"You have brains in your head. You have feet in your shoes. You can steer yourself any direction you choose. You're on your own. And you know what you know. And you are the one who'll decide where to go..." –Dr. Seuss, Oh, the Places You'll Go!

The Rich Treasure

Once there was a farmer who had four sons. The farmer was a hard-working man, but his sons were very lazy. As the farmer grew old, he realized that he had to teach his sons the value of hard work before he died. So, he took all his money and bought some land. The land was covered with weeds and full of stones, but the man knew it would be fertile ground for farming. His sons, however, were angry because they thought the land was worthless. They complained bitterly, but their father promised them that he had a good reason for buying the land.

Then, when he grew sick and knew he was dying, he summoned his sons and revealed the secret. "Now, before it is too late, I will tell you why I bought that land. The goddess Fortuna appeared to me and told me that in that land there is a treasure chest full of gold, but it is buried deep within the ground. Just find the buried treasure, and you will be wealthy for the rest of your lives." With those words, the old man died.

The sons were eager to uncover the treasure, so they started to dig. They pulled up the weeds and carted away the stones, turning over the soil to look for the treasure. They worked the ground for many days finding no gold but eventually understanding their father's words: the treasure was the land itself, made rich by their own hard work. They planted crops and the harvest was plentiful, and so it was every year, just as their father had promised.

The moral of the story is that hard work pays off, although it is not always in the way that you expect!

Affirmation: My hard work pays off.

To think about:

1. How much satisfaction do your receive from working hard?

2. How could your hard work pay off in ways you do not expect?

3. Do you measure wealth by your material possessions or the satisfaction present in your life?

The price of success is hard work, dedication to the job at hand, and the determination that whether we win or lose, we have applied the best of ourselves to the task at hand.
-Vince Lombardi

The Old Man and the Children

A group of children were playing, loud and noisy in front of an old man's house. The old man, after a while, couldn't stand it any more. He walked out and handed 25 cents to each child and said, "You guys made my place not so lonely any more. I feel much younger. Take these as my gratitude."

The children were very happy and came back to play loudly the next day. The old man came out and handed each of them 15 cents. He explained, "I don't have much income. 15 cents is not bad at all." The children were satisfied and left.

The next day, he only gave them 5 cents each.

The children were upset, "Only 5 cents?! Have you no idea how hard we were playing for you!" Then they swore they were never going to play for the old man again.

The old man in the story converted, rather cleverly, the children's motivation to play from an internal one, "playing for fun," to an external one, "playing for the money."

Affirmation: The satisfaction of a task well done motivates me.

To think about:

1. How do external rewards motivate you?

2. What motivates you internally?

3. Which do you have more control over, the external or internal motivation?

People often say that motivation doesn't last. Well, neither does bathing—that's why we recommend it daily. -Zig Ziglar

Destiny

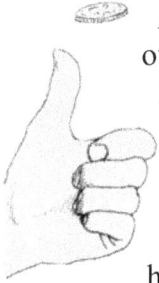

A Japanese general was in the middle of a monumental battle. His army was greatly outnumbered and his men were filled with doubt. The general made the decision that he would attack. On the way to the battle, they stopped at a religious shrine to pray. After prayer, the general took out a coin and said "I shall now toss this coin. If it is heads, we shall win. If tails, we shall lose. Destiny will now reveal itself."

He threw the coin into the air with all the men watching intently as it landed. It was heads. The soldiers were so fired up and filled with confidence that they ferociously attacked the enemy and were victorious. After the battle, a lieutenant remarked to the general, "No one can change destiny."

"You are right," the general replied as he showed the lieutenant the coin, which had heads on both sides.

Affirmation: A positive attitude and great effort determine my destiny.

To think about:

1. Can you change your destiny?

2. If you aren't responsible for yourself, who will be?

3. How does a confidence and belief in yourself lead to success?

Believe in yourself, and the rest will fall into place. Have faith in your own abilities, work hard, and there is nothing you cannot accomplish. -Brad Henry

The Road Not Taken

Two roads diverged in a yellow wood,
And sorry I could not travel both
And be one traveler, long I stood
And looked down one as far as I could
To where it bent in the undergrowth.

Then took the other, as just as fair,
And having perhaps the better claim,
Because it was grassy and wanted wear;
Though as for that the passing there
Had worn them really about the same.

And both that morning equally lay
In leaves no step had trodden black.
Oh, I kept the first for another day!
Yet knowing how way leads on to way,
I doubted if I should ever come back.

I shall be telling this with a sigh
Somewhere ages and ages hence:
Two roads diverged in a wood, and I--
I took the one less traveled by,
And that has made all the difference.

—Robert Frost

People have to make tough choices when traveling the road of life. What is often the most popular choice is not always the right choice.

Affirmation: I take the road less traveled, and it makes all the difference.

To think about:

1. When you have to make a difficult choice, what do you rely on to help you make the choice?

2. How can taking the road less traveled make all the difference?

3. How do you feel when you know you have made the right choice?

Some choices we live not only once but a thousand times over, remembering them for the rest of our lives. -Richard Bach

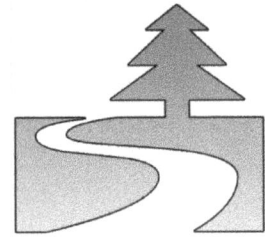

Little Fellow Follows Me

A careful man I ought to be, A little fellow follows me. I dare not go astray, for fear he'll go the self-same way. I cannot once escape his eyes, Whatever he see me do, he tries. Like me, he says, he's going to be, The little chap who follows me. He thinks that I am good and fine, Believes in every word of mine. The base in me he must not see, That little fellow who follows me. I must remember as I go, Thru summers' sun and winters' snow. I am building for the years to be, In the little chap who follows me. -- Author Unknown

Has it ever occurred to you that you may be a role model to someone else such as a teammate, friend, or younger child? People are always watching you, even if you are not aware of it. The more you do what's right, the more you are a positive role model. Athletes need to possess the best characteristics of both an athlete and a person, including integrity, honesty, generosity, perseverance, sportsmanship, and the pursuit of excellence.

When you have a vision of doing something special with your life and work toward that vision, you will become a positive role model for others. What you value, believe in, and respect will determine how positive of a role model you are.

Being a role model isn't always easy. There will be times when you will find yourself at odds with your friends. You'll even worry about fitting in. But don't worry.

Being a role model means that you stand out for others to see. A role model is someone who chooses to put forth their best effort every day, and when they make a mistake they pick themselves up and try again. Athletes need to be held to higher standards than the average person as they become good role models for young students and children in the community.

Affirmation: I lead by example.

To think about:

1. Are you a positive role model?

2. If you are a positive role model, why do you believe you are? If you do not consider yourself a positive role model, what can you do to become one?

3. What challenges do you face in being a positive role model?

Nothing is so infectious as example. -Francois de LaRochefoucaul

Water Bearer and the Pots

A water bearer in India had two large pots, each hanging on one end of a pole which he slung across the back of his neck. One pot was perfect and always maintained a full pot of water at the end of the long walk home from the stream. The other pot had a crack in it and always arrived at the master's house only half full.

For a full two years, the routine went on daily, with the water bearer delivering only one and a half pots full of water to his master's house. The perfect pot was proud of its accomplishments, but the cracked pot was ashamed that it was able to accomplish only half of what it had been made to do.

Finally, the cracked pot spoke to the water bearer one day by the stream. "I am ashamed of myself, and I must apologize to you. I have long been able to deliver only half my load, because this crack in my side causes water to leak out all the way back to your master's house," the pot answered. "Because of my flaws, you have to do all of this work, and you don't get full value from your efforts."

The water bearer felt sorry for the old cracked pot, and compassionately said, "As we return to the master's house today, I want you to notice something: the beautiful flowers along the way."

So as they went up the hill, the old cracked pot took notice of how the sun warmed scores of beautiful wildflowers on the side of the path, and this vision cheered it some. But at the end of the trail, the pot still felt bad because once again it had leaked out half its load—and thus once again it apologized to the water bearer for its perceived failings.

The water bearer said to the cracked pot, "Did you happen to notice that there were flowers only on your side of the path, and not on the other pot's side? That's because I have always known about your flaw, and I took advantage of it. I planted flower seeds on your side of the path, and every day while we have walked back from the stream, you've watered them. For two years I have been able to pick these beautiful flowers to decorate my master's table. If you were not just as you are, he would not have such beauty to grace his house."

Affirmation: I accept my imperfection and strive to improve.

To think about:

1. We all have flaws, but it is important to recognize that the flaws have potential benefits. What benefits may your flaws have?

2. How can we use our weaknesses, to discover our strengths?

3. Have you had flaws that turned into strengths?

Perhaps I am stronger than I think. -Thomas Merton

You Can Make a Difference

While walking along a beach, an elderly gentleman saw someone in the distance leaning down, picking something up and throwing it into the ocean. As he got closer, he noticed that the figure was that of a young man, picking up starfish one by one and tossing each one gently back into the water.

He came closer still and called out, "Good morning! May I ask what it is that you are doing?" the young man paused, looked up, and replied "Throwing starfish into the ocean."

The old man smiled, and said, "I must ask, then, why are you throwing starfish into the ocean?"

To this, the young man replied, "The sun is up and the tide is going out. If I don't throw them in, they'll die."

Upon hearing this, the elderly observer commented, "But, young man, do you not realize that there are miles and miles of beach and there are starfish all along every mile? You can't possibly make a difference!"

The young man listened politely. Then he bent down, picked up another starfish, threw it into the back into the ocean past the breaking waves and said, *"It made a difference for that one."*

Affirmation: I am making a difference.

To think about:

1. What does the term "make a difference" mean to you?

2. Do you ever feel like your efforts are being wasted? Reflect on how your efforts may be important to someone.

3. How can you make a difference in others' lives?

One person can make a difference, and everyone should try." -John F. Kennedy

Touchstone

When the great library of Alexandria burned, one book was saved. It was not a valuable book so a poor man, who could read a little, bought it for a few coppers. The book wasn't very interesting, but between its pages there was something very interesting indeed. It was a thin strip of vellum on which was written the secret of the "Touchstone."

The touchstone was a small pebble that could turn any common metal into pure gold. The writing explained that it was lying among thousands and thousands of other pebbles that looked exactly like it. The secret was that the real stone would feel warm, while ordinary pebbles are cold.

So the man sold his few belongings, bought some simple supplies, camped on the seashore, and began testing pebbles. He knew that if he picked up ordinary pebbles and threw them down again because they were cold, he might pick up the same pebble hundreds of times. So, when he felt one that was cold, he threw it into the sea. He spent a whole day doing this but none of them was the touchstone, yet he went on and on this way.

Pick up a pebble. Cold - throw it into the sea. Pick up another. Throw it into the sea. The days stretched into weeks and the weeks into months. One day, however, he picked up a pebble and it was warm. He threw it into the sea before he realized what he had done. He had formed such a strong habit of throwing each pebble into the sea that when the one he wanted came along, he still threw it away.

It is the same way with opportunity. Unless we are vigilant, it is easy to fail to recognize an opportunity when it is in hand and it is just as easy to throw it away.

Affirmation: I develop good habits.

To think about:

1. Think of three bad habits you have. How did you develop those habits?

2. If you developed bad habits, how do you break them?

3. Think of three good habits you have. How did you develop those habits?

We are what we repeatedly do. Excellence, then, is not an act, but a habit. -Aristotle

The Precious Present

This is a story about a little boy, an old man and the wisdom that comes with age. The old man told the boy, "You have a great gift, it's called the *The Precious Present,* and it's the best present a person can receive because anyone who receives such a gift is happy forever. "

"Wow!" the little boy said. "I hope someone gives me *The Precious Present* for Christmas."

As the years passed, the boy would approach the old man to ask him again and again about the great gift. He couldn't figure out what the *Precious Present* was. He knew It had to be something special, because the old man had said it would bring happiness forever.

As the years went by and the boy became a young man, he became increasingly annoyed that he had never gotten The Precious Present as a child. "If you want me to be happy," the young man shouted, "why don't you just tell me what *The Precious Present* is?"

"And where to find it," the old man said. "I would like to, but I do not have such powers. No one does. Only you have the power to make yourself happy. "

The young man began a life-long quest for *The Precious Present.* He read books and looked near and far. But he never found *The Precious Present.*

Finally, after many years, when he became an old man, it hit him what *The Precious Present* is. It is just that- the present. Not the past and not the future, but *The Precious Present.* It's the ability to live in the present tense.

We often become obsessed with a loss or a failure and let it consume us. We become focused on yesterday and the mistakes of the past, or we believe the future will be much better.

Affirmation: I am focused on the present.

To think about:

1. How do you focus to stay "in the present?"

2. How does your focus on the past or on the future, hinder you from reaching your goals?

3. What are the rewards of *The Precious Present?*

The sun focused through a magnifying glass can start a fire. Focus is so powerful. -Unknown

Lifting Calf

Milo was born over 2,000 years ago in an ancient Greek colony of southern Italy, and grew up to win the Olympic wrestling championship six times. It was reported that his strength was so great that when a building collapsed, he supported the roof while his friends were able to escape unharmed.

The mythical story of how Milo got his strength has been told for over 2,000 years. When he was a boy, his father gave a newborn bull calf to Milo. Milo lifted the calf in his arms and carried it on his back every day. He continued the exercise every day and his strength grew, along with his calf. One day, his father asked him, "How big is your bull today?" Milo ran outside, picked up the calf and carried him inside to show his father. Each day, his father asked him, "How big is your bull today?" and each day Milo ran outside, picked up the bull and carried him to his father. This went on for a number of years and Milo could easily lift it in his arms even when it grew into an adult bull. This enabled him to become an athlete of unparalleled strength and stamina.

The story of Milo's successful training teaches us a lesson in development. In today's society, we tend to be impatient and want things immediately. In Milo terminology, we want the calf to grow up quickly into a cow. It takes time and patience for our body to make the physiological changes as we train. We can't expect the calf to grow into a cow overnight, and we can't expect our body to reach maximal development overnight. If we follow a proper training program, follow nutritional guidelines, and avoid illegal drugs, our body will respond to our training. Be patient, keep working hard and doing the right things and your body will respond and progress.

Affirmation: I work hard and smart to get better every day.

To think about:

1. Do you have a "want it now" attitude? Good things take time to develop. What things could you do to focus on being patient?

2. Think back over the last 5-10 years on the progress you have made.

3. Look down the road 5-10 years. Where do you see yourself at that time? What will it take to get there?

Every day do something that will inch you closer to a better tomorrow. -Doug Firebaugh

Never Quit-Bamboo

One day a farmer planted fern and bamboo seeds in the ground. The farmer took very good care of them. He made sure they had water and sunlight to grow.

The fern quickly grew from the earth with a brilliant color. Nothing came from the bamboo seed. However, the farmer continued to nurture both the fern and bamboo seeds with water and sunlight.

In the second year, the fern continued to grow healthy. Nothing came from the bamboo seed.

In the third year, there was still nothing from the bamboo seed. In the fourth year, again, there was nothing from the bamboo seed, but the farmer continued to nurture the seed.

In the fifth year, a tiny sprout emerged from the earth. Compared to the fern, it was seemingly small and insignificant. But the bamboo grew very quickly to a foot high, then two and three and in just six months the bamboo had risen to over 100 feet tall.

It had spent five years growing roots. Those roots made it strong and gave it what it needed to survive. All the time the bamboo seed appeared to be struggling, it was actually growing roots.

Don't compare yourself to others. The bamboo had a different purpose than the fern. Yet, they both make the forest beautiful

Be patient as you grow roots. Your time will come to rise high!

Affirmation: I grow as a person every day.

To think about:

1. What will you need to do to develop strong roots?

2. If you keep growing roots and are patient, your time will come. How will you be patient?

3. Growing a little bit everyday adds up. List five ways that you grow daily.

Have a strong will, not a strong won't. -Unknown

Woodcutter

Once upon a time there was a man traveling through a forest who came upon a woodcutter hard at work. The man could see that the woodcutter was a powerful and dedicated tradesman.

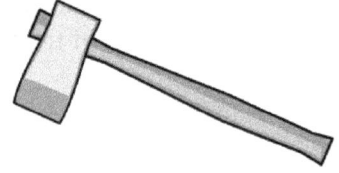

The traveler tried to engage the woodcutter in conversation, but the woodcutter was too busy to be disturbed. Huffing and puffing, he said to the traveler, "I don't mean to be rude sir, but I must keep working or I will not get this wood finished on time." The woodcutter cut down 18 trees that first day.

The next day, the traveler came by and saw that the woodcutter was indeed cutting a lot of wood, but he was expending so much effort doing it. Although the woodcutter was trying hard, he only cut down 15 trees the second day.

The next day, the traveler came by and noticed the woodcutter had only brought down 10 trees on the third day.

It was then the traveler noticed that the woodcutter's axe seemed somewhat dull and rusty. He asked the woodcutter "Why don't you stop and sharpen your axe?"

The woodcutter kept chopping and huffing and said "Don't be ridiculous! How can I take the time to sharpen my axe when I have so much wood to cut!"

Affirmation: I take the time to properly prepare.

To think about:

1. Are you often too busy to take the time and sharpen your axe and prepare properly?

2. How do you keep an overall view of your main goal?

3. What does it mean to "try smarter, not harder?"

Success depends upon previous preparation, and without such preparation there is sure to be failure. -Confucius

Stonecutter

Stone cutters process or shape crude and rough pieces of rocks into desirable shape, sizes and patterns for the purpose of building and creating structures. Stone cutting is an occupation that has existed since the dawn of civilization. Stone masonry was born when people began fashioning homes for themselves built with mud, straw, or stone. During the Neolithic Age, people learned how to use fire and subsequently created quicklime, mortars, and plasters. By using these to cement stones together, they went on to create buildings, structures, and sculptures.. Throughout the ages, these impressive works of architecture and engineering of the ancient world were heavily dependent upon the work of stone masons. From the Egyptian and Mayan pyramids, to the Persian palaces and Greek temples and down to the Roman Coliscum, stone masonry made a significant contribution of to these engineering marvels.

The stone cutter hammers away at the stone, driving his hammer into the chisel in at attempt to cut the stone. He may hammer away a hundred times without as much as a crack showing in it. But, at the hundred and first blow it will split in two. It was not the final blow that did it, but all that had gone before.

Affirmation: I persistently work toward my target.

To think about:

1. How does the story of cutting the stone apply to the tasks you take on?

2. Have you ever felt like you were not making any progress?

3. What does it mean to put in the proper preparation?

A little more persistence, a little more effort, and what seemed hopeless failure may turn to glorious success. -Elbert Hubbard

More Is Not Always Better

Once upon a time there was a stone cutter. He was not satisfied with his life. As he passed by a wealthy merchant's house one day he saw how many fine possessions the merchant had. He wished that he could be like the merchant. Amazingly, his dream came true. He became the rich and powerful merchant. One day, he saw a high official being carried in a chair, accompanied by attendants and solders. Everyone was bowing to the official. The official was the centerpiece of a parade. How powerful that official is!" he thought. "I wish that I could be a high official!"

Amazingly, he became the high official, carried everywhere in his embroidered chair, but feared and hated by the people all around. As it was a hot summer day, he felt very uncomfortable in the chair. As he looked up at the sun, he thought, "How powerful the sun is, I wish that I could be the sun!"

Amazingly, he became the sun, shining fiercely down on everyone, scorching the fields, cursed by the all farmers. Soon a huge black cloud moved between him and the earth, so that his light could no longer shine on everything below. "How powerful that storm cloud is!" he thought. "I wish that I could be a cloud!"

Amazingly, he became the cloud, and flooded the fields and villages, shouted at by everyone. But soon he found that he was being pushed away by a great force, and realized that it was the wind. "How powerful it is!" he thought. "I wish that I could be the wind!"

Amazingly, he became the wind, blowing tiles off the roofs of houses, uprooting trees, feared and hated by all below him. But he came up against something that would not move, no matter how forcefully he blew against it - a huge, towering rock. "How powerful that rock is!" he thought. "I wish that I could be a rock!"

Amazingly, he became the rock, more powerful than anything else on earth. But as he stood there, he heard the sound of a hammer pounding a chisel into the hard surface, and felt himself being changed. "What could be more powerful than I, the rock?" he thought. As he looked around, he saw the figure of a stone cutter.

Affirmation: I am happy with life.

To think about:

1. What great power do you have within you?

2. Do you jump from one desire to the next, never content with how things really are?

3. How can you celebrate who you are and what you stand for?

We often meet our destiny on the road we took to avoid it. -Unknown

Echo of the Mountain

A son and his father were walking on the mountains.
Suddenly, his son falls, hurts himself and screams: "AAAhhhhhhhhhhh!!!"
To his surprise, he hears the voice repeating, somewhere in the mountain:
"AAAhhhhhhhhhhh!!!"
Curious, he yells: "Who are you?"
He receives the answer: "Who are you?"
And then he screams to the mountain: "I admire you!"
The voice answers: "I admire you!"
Angered at the response, he screams: "Coward!"
He receives the answer: "Coward!"
He looks to his father and asks: "What's going on?"
The father smiles and says: "My son, pay attention."
Again the man screams: "You are a champion!"
The voice answers: "You are a champion!"
The boy is surprised, but does not understand.
Then the father explains: "People call this ECHO, but really this is LIFE.
It gives you back everything you say or do.
Our life is simply a reflection of our actions.
If you want more love in the world, create more love in your heart.
If you want more competence in your team, improve your competence.
This relationship applies to everything, in all aspects of life.
Life will give you back everything you have given to it."

--Unknown Author

Affirmation: I think positive thoughts.

To think about:

1. What percent of the time do you think positive thoughts? What percent of the time do you think negative thoughts? Your answer should add up to 100 percent.

2. Your thoughts help determine your actions and who you are. How do your actions reflect who you are?

3. What do you give back to life?

Whether you think you can or think you can't, you're right. -Henry Ford

Garbage Truck

A man hopped in a taxi and took off for the airport. All of a sudden, a car came out of a parking spot and pulled right in front of the taxi. The taxi driver slammed on his brakes, skidding and just missed running into the other car. The driver of the car who had almost caused the accident was very unhappy and started cussing. The taxi driver just smiled and waved at the guy.

The passenger in the taxi was amazed and said, "Why did you just do that? This guy almost ruined your car and sent us to the hospital." That's when the taxi driver explained "The Law of the Garbage Truck."

Many people are like garbage trucks. They run around full of garbage, full of frustration, full of anger, and full of disappointment. As their garbage piles up, they need a place to dump it. And if you let them, they'll dump it on you. When someone wants to dump on you, don't take it personally. Just smile, wave, wish them well, and move on. You'll be happy you did.

Affirmation: I am always positive.

To think about:

1. How often do you let "garbage trucks" run over you?

2. How often do you take other people's garbage and spread it to other people?

3. What would happen in your life, starting today, if you let more garbage trucks pass you by?

Do the best you can, where you are, with what you have. -Unknown

Giant Slayer

The Israeli and Philistine armies faced each other for battle. The Philistine army had a soldier that was a giant of a man, Goliath, who reportedly stood nine feet tall. The army from Israel was terrified of Goliath and no one wanted to meet him in battle.

But surprisingly, there was a volunteer from Israel willing to fight against Goliath. He was a young shepherd named David. The king agreed to send him to the war against Goliath.

David went to the war without a sword or any armor. He carried simple shepherd tools such as a slingshot and a pouch of stones, but the biggest weapon he had was his trust in God and self-confidence.

When they met on the battlefield, Goliath thought it was funny that David was going to battle him. David reached into his bag, and with his slingshot, slung a stone onto Goliath's head. The stone sailed directly into Goliath's forehead, finding a spot where Goliath had no armor. Goliath fell to the ground, killed by a stone from the brave shepherd. The death of Goliath weakened the Philistines and lead to an Israel victory.

While the Israel army saw Goliath as unbeatable, David looked at Goliath as just another human being. Even though David was an underdog, he did not focus on the size of his opponent; he focused on his abilities and what he was capable of doing.

Affirmation: I focus on what I am capable of doing.

To think about:

1. Do you allow giants in your life to become so big that they block out your view of anything else?

2. Do you allow problems to turn into giants? What is the attitude you need to have in order to slay your giants? 3. Are there challenges that others are afraid to take on?

3. Are you willing to take that challenge?

Focus on the negative and you will stumble, but focus on the positive and the negatives will tumble. -Unknown

The Twenty Dollar Bill

One day in class the teacher held up a $20 bill and asked, "Who would like this $20 bill?"

Hands started going up. He said, "I am going to give this $20 to one of you, but first, let me do this." He proceeded to crumple the dollar bill up. He then asked, "Who still wants it?" Still, the hands were up in the air.

"Well," he replied, "what if I do this?" He dropped it on the ground and started to grind it into the floor with his shoe. He picked it up, now crumpled and dirty. "Now who still wants it?" Still, the hands went into the air.

No matter what the teacher did to the money, people still wanted it because it did not decrease in value. It was still worth $20.

Many times in our lives, we are dropped, crumpled, and ground into the dirt by the decisions we make and the circumstances that come our way. We may feel as though we are worthless, but no matter what has happened or what will happen, we never lose our value as a person.

Affirmation: I learn from failure.

To think about:

1. Do you tie your self-worth into your performance?

2. Are you still the same person you were before a bad performance?

3. Think of 10 things you do well outside of an athletic performance.

Success is never final, failure is never fatal. -John Wooden

Chicken and the Hen

Once upon a time, a man found an eagle's egg. He took it home and placed it under one of his brooding hens. The eaglet hatched with the chickens and as he grew up with the chickens he grew to be like them. He clucked and cackled. He scratched the earth for worms. He flapped his wings and managed to fly just a few feet in the air.

As the years went by, the eagle continued to live with the chickens. The eagle had now grown old. As he looked to the sky he saw a magnificent bird flying high above him in the sky. He noticed how the beautiful bird was gracefully gliding against the powerful wind, its golden wings effortlessly moving. The eagle was awed by the majestic nature of the magnificent bird and asked, "Who's that?"

"That's the king of the birds, the eagle," said a chicken. "He belongs to the sky. We belong to earth, we're chickens."

So the eagle lived his life as a chicken for that's what he thought he was.'

Affirmation: I soar with the eagles.

To think about:

1. How can your thoughts limit your performance?

2. How can your environment limit your performance?

3. What does it take to break out of limiting thoughts?

Dare to live the life you have dreamed for yourself. Go forward and make your dreams come true. -Ralph Waldo Emerson

Positive Thoughts Lead to Positive Words

A monk went into a monastery that was very strict. The monks took a vow of silence and with only one small exception they were not allowed to speak at all. Every ten years, the monks were allowed to speak just two words. Ten years went by at the monastery and the monk was brought to the head monk. It has been ten years," said the head monk. "What are the two words you would like to speak?" "Bed... hard..." said the monk.

"I see," replied the head monk. Ten more years passed before the monk was returned to the head monk's office again. "It has been ten more years," said the head monk. "What are the two words you would like to speak? "Food... stinks..." said the monk.

"I see," replied the head monk. Another ten years passed and the monk once again met with the head monk who asked, "What are your two words now, after these ten years?" I... quit!" said the monk.

"Well, I can see why," replied the head monk. "All you ever do is complain."

Affirmation: I choose to be positive.

To think about:

1. We can choose to focus on the positive aspects of our lives or dwell of the negatives. Compare how much can be accomplished between the two?

2. Which is more fun?

3. Is being negative contagious? Is being positive contagious?

The pessimist sees difficulty in every opportunity. The optimist sees the opportunity in every difficulty. -Winston Churchill

Seed

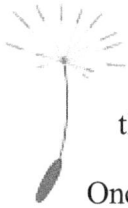

A flower seed can sit on a store shelf in a package and lay for years without any life in it. However, when that seed gets planted in the ground, a metamorphosis takes place. It starts to germinate and open. It starts to spread open, and against all odds the tiny little seed pushes through dirt to break through the ground to grow.

Once the seed is placed in the right environment and in the right soil with water and sunlight, the seed will flourish. What was once a dormant and unproductive seed grows into a beautiful flower.

We can be like that package of seed in the store, always sitting around with our potential laying lifeless inside, waiting to show our potential, but do not for some reason or another.

Or we can be like the seed that gets planted and begins to flourish. In order for our full potential to come out from within, we need to be in the right environment so that we can flourish. Our soil needs to be perfect so that we can germinate. We need to be near positive people with motivation to succeed; people with plans to achieve their goals and dreams, who strive for success on a daily basis.

We have the same ability as that beautiful flower that continues to grow every year. It is our choice. You can plant yourself and grow to your potential if you plant yourself in the right environment, or you can sit in the pouch with all the rest of the seeds on a shelf in the store.

Choose to be planted and grow every day. Nourish yourself with fresh thoughts and look forward to improving yourself daily.

Affirmation: With the help of others, I grow every day.

To think about:

1. What type of environment should you seek to be able to grow?

2. List some people that could help you achieve your goals.

3. How will you seek and use these people to be able to establish a positive growing environment?

Ninety-five percent of people never succeed because they're following the wrong group. -Earl Nightingale

Attitude of Gratitude

Gratitude is defined as being appreciative of what you have. If you consistently recognize everything that you have, you will be a happier person. However, gratitude is not durable and must be reinforced daily. Grateful people may be thought of as those who always see the glass as half full while ungrateful people see the same glass as half-empty.

"Thank you."

Do you have money in the bank, in your wallet or spare change in a cup someplace? If you do, you are among the top eight percent of the world's wealthiest people.

Did you wake up this morning with more health than illness? If so, you are more blessed than the million people who will die this week.

Have you ever experienced the danger of battle, the loneliness of prison, the agony of torture, or the pangs of starvation? If not, you are ahead of 20 million people in the world.

Do you have food in the refrigerator, clothes on your back, a roof over your head and a place to sleep? If so, you are richer than 75 percent of the people in this world.

If you can read this message, you are more blessed than more than two billion people in the world who cannot read anything at all.

If you hold your head up with a smile on your face and are truly thankful, you are blessed, because the majority of people can, but most do not.

We often take for granted the most important things we are blessed to have and the people that make a difference in our life. Take time to think about what you are grateful for. Developing an attitude of gratitude will make you a happier, more productive person.

Affirmation: I have an attitude of gratitude.

To think about:

1. What are the characteristics of a grateful person?

2. Why is it important to be grateful?

3. Why doesn't gratitude last?

Gratitude is when memory is stored in the heart and not in the mind. -Lionel Hampton

Build Your Best House

A carpenter was at the end of a long and successful career and decided to retire. He wanted to enjoy retirement by spending more time with his wife and family. He liked drawing the paycheck of a successful carpenter but he longed to retire and felt his family could get by on the money he had saved. He informed his employer of his plans to retire.

His employer was sorry to see the carpenter retire as he had been a good worker. The employer persuaded the carpenter to build just one more house as a personal favor. However, as the carpenter started building his final house, he soon found out that his heart was not in his work. He did not use his normal quality workmanship and he cut corners by using inferior materials. It was an unfortunate way to end the carpenter's career by building a house far below his usual high standards. When the carpenter finished his work and the builder came to inspect the house, the employer handed the front door key to the carpenter.

"This is your house," his employer said, "my gift to you." If only the carpenter had known he was building his own house, he would have done it all so differently. Now, he had to live in the home he had shabbily built.

Think of yourself as the carpenter. Each day you live is like building a house. However, your life is the only life you will ever build. Do you give each day your best effort? Or are you building the house that you want to live in?

Affirmation: I have complete control over my attitude and effort.

To think about:

1. Have you ever looked back on something and realized you would have done it differently if you could do it over?

2. How is your life today a result of your attitudes and choices in the past?

3. How will your life tomorrow be the result of your attitudes and the choices you make today? What control do you have over the life you build?

Quality is not an act, it is a habit. -Aristotle

Are You a Team Goose?

When you see geese heading south for the winter flying along in the "V" formation, you might be interested in knowing what science has discovered about why they fly that way. It has been discovered that as each bird flaps its wings, it creates uplift for the bird immediately following. By flying in a "V" formation, the whole flock adds at least 71 percent greater flying range than if each bird flew on its own.

People who are part of a team share a common direction and get where they are going more quickly and easily, because they are traveling on the trust of one another. Whenever a goose falls out of formation, it suddenly feels the drag and resistance of trying to fly alone and quickly gets back into formation to take advantage of the power of the flock. When the lead goose gets tired, they rotate back in the wing and another goose takes over. The geese honk from behind to encourage those up front to keep their speed. Words of support and inspiration help energize teammates, helping them to keep pace in spite of challenges.

When a goose gets sick or hurt and falls out of formation, two geese fall out of the formation and follow the injured one down to help and protect them. They stay with them until the injured goose is either able to fly or until they are dead, and then they launch out with another formation to catch up with their group.

If we take lessons from a goose, we will stand by each other when things get rough.
The next time you see a formation of geese, remember: It is a "privilege" to be a contributing member of a team.

Affirmation: I add power to my team.

To think about:

1. What do you bring to the team that makes the team better?

2. What do you get from the team that makes you better?

3. What sacrifices are you willing to make for the team?

When a team outgrows individual performance and learns team confidence, excellence becomes a reality. -Joe Paterno

Blind Boy

A blind boy sat on the steps of a building with a hat by his feet. He held up a sign which said: "I am blind, please help." There were only a few coins in the hat.

A man was walking by. He took a few coins from his pocket and dropped them into the hat. He then took the sign, turned it around and wrote some words. He put the sign back so that everyone who walked by would see the new words

Soon the hat began to fill up. A lot more people were giving money to the blind boy.

That afternoon, the man who had changed the sign came to see how things were. The boy recognized his footsteps and asked, "Were you the one who changed my sign this morning? What did you write?"

The man said, "I only wrote the truth. I said what you said but in a different way."

What he had written was, "Today is a beautiful day and I cannot see it."

Of course both signs told people the boy was blind. But the first sign simply said the boy was blind. The second sign told people they were so lucky that they were not blind.

Be thankful for what you have. Be creative. Be innovative. Be positive.

Affirmation: I see things in a positive way.

To think about:

1. When you hear something that sounds negative, how do you respond?

2. When you hear something that sounds positive, how do you respond?

3. Think of a day when you were thinking positive. List five examples of how things turned out great because of your positive attitude.

The positive thinker sees the invisible, feels the intangible, and achieves the impossible.
-Winston Churchill

Growing Good Corn

There was a Nebraska farmer who grew award-winning corn. Each year he entered his corn in the state fair, where it won a blue ribbon. One year, a newspaper reporter interviewed him and learned something interesting about how he grew it. The reporter discovered that the farmer shared his seed corn with his neighbors.

"How can you afford to share your best seed corn with your neighbors when they are entering corn in competition with yours each year?" the reporter asked.

"Why sir," said the farmer, "didn't you know? The wind picks up pollen from the ripening corn and swirls it from field to field. If my neighbors grow inferior corn, cross-pollination will steadily degrade the quality of my corn. If I am to grow good corn, I must help my neighbors grow good corn. My corn cannot improve unless my neighbor's corn also improves."

People who want to improve must help other people improve, also. Those who choose to make a commitment must help others to make a commitment. The value of a life is measured by the lives it touches. Those who desire to be successful must help others to find success, for the success of each is tied to the success of all.

The lesson is this: if we are to grow good corn, we must help our teammates grow good corn.

Affirmation: I help make my teammates better and they make me better.

To think about:

1. Think of a time that you made a teammate better. What did you do? How did you feel?

2. Think of a time when a teammate made you better. What did they do? How did you feel?

3. What can you do to help improve your teammates?

The achievements of an organization are the results of the combined effort of each individual.
-Vince Lombardi

Rabbit and the Turtle Race

You've heard the story about the rabbit and the turtle. The rabbit started off very fast using its speed. Meanwhile, the slow moving rabbit consistently moved down the course. Way ahead and feeling very confident, the rabbit felt tired so he lay down to take a nap. The turtle continued to slowly move down the course and passed the napping rabbit and went on to win the race.

The rabbit wanted a rematch. This time, he decided, he would not take a nap. When the race started, the rabbit hopped off quickly, did not stop to take a nap this time, and defeated the turtle quiet easily. Next time, the turtle challenged the rabbit to a rematch on a different course. The rabbit knew the reason he had lost the first race was because he was lazy. He was able to win the second race because he put some work into it. He was confident he would win the third race, so he accepted the challenge.

When the third race started, the rabbit took off fast and disappeared. He wanted to defeat the turtle by a larger margin than the earlier race. When he came to a river on the course, he was not able to figure out how to cross it and had to stop. Later, the turtle reached the river and stepped right into it. The turtle crossed the finished line while the rabbit helplessly looked on as the turtle won the race. The rabbit realized that that being faster is not enough; one should have brains as well to complete the task. The rabbit and the turtle decided to run again. Not race, just run.

As they started off running, the rabbit put the turtle on his back until they reached the river. Once they needed to cross the river, the turtle put the rabbit on his back. After crossing the river, the rabbit again put the turtle on his back, and both of them reached the finishing line in less time than ever. When the rabbit and the turtle were competing against one another, only one was able win, with both wasting time and energy. With teamwork, you can finish the same task quicker with everyone able to enjoy the reward.

Affirmation: I am a great teammate.

To think about:

1. How can you work with your teammates to be more productive?

2. Think of ways in the past that you have worked with your teammates to have fun. What future ways can you have fun with your teammates as you work toward a goal?

3. How does the story relate to the saying, "Together Everyone Achieves More."

Teamwork is the ability to work together toward a common vision. The ability to direct individual accomplishments toward organizational objectives. It is the fuel that allows common people to attain uncommon results. -Andrew Carnegie

Ultimate Sacrifice

An 8-year-old boy had a younger sister who was dying of leukemia, and he was told that without a blood transfusion, she would die. His parents explained to him that his blood was probably compatible with hers, and if so, could he be the blood donor. They asked him if they could test his blood and he said sure. After testing the blood, they found it was a good match. Then they asked if he would give his sister a pint of blood, that it could be her only chance of living. He said he would have to think about it overnight.

The next day, he went to his parents and said he was willing to donate the blood. So they took him to the hospital where he was placed in a bed beside his 6-year-old sister, and both of them were hooked up to IVs. A nurse withdrew a pint of blood from the boy, which was then put in the girl's IV. The boy lay in silence, while the blood dripped into his sister, until the doctor came over to see how he was doing. The boy opened his eyes and asked. "How soon until I start to die?"

The young boy had thought that giving blood to his sister would kill him, but he was willing to die for her.

Affirmations: I am willing to make sacrifice to make others better.

To think about:

1. What are you willing to sacrifice for the people around you?

2. How can you make the people around you better?

3. How can people around you make you better?

Great achievement is usually born of sacrifice, and is never the result of selfishness.
-Napolean Hill

Warwick the Mule

A man was lost while driving through the country. As he tried to reach for the map, he accidentally drove off the road into a ditch. Though he wasn't injured, his car was stuck deep in the mud. So the man walked to a nearby farm to ask for help.

"Warwick can get you out of that ditch," said the farmer, pointing to an old mule standing in a field. The man looked at the decrepit old mule and looked at the farmer who just stood there repeating, "Yep, old Warwick can do the job." The man figured he had nothing to lose. The two men and the mule made their way back to the ditch. The farmer hitched the mule to the car. With a snap of the reins he shouted:

"Pull, Fred! Pull, Jack! Pull, Ted! Pull, Warwick!"

And the mule pulled that car right out of the ditch. The man was amazed. He thanked the farmer, patted the mule, and asked, "Why did you call out all of those names before you called Warwick?"

What did the farmer reply?

The farmer grinned and said, "Old Warwick is just about blind. As long as he believes he's part of a team, he doesn't mind pulling."

Affirmation: My teammates make me better.

To think about:

1. How can the team make you better?

2. What can you contribute to benefit the team?

3. How can the whole be greater than the sum of the parts?

It is amazing how much you can accomplish when it doesn't matter who gets the credit.
-Harry Truman

Resources

The Butterfly
   Author Unknown

Buzzard, Bat and Bumblebee
   The Buzzard, Bat and Bumblebee. http://message.snopes.com/showthread.php?t=34551

Eagles in a Storm
   Monroe, M., *7 Principles of an Eagle.* http://sharelife.wordpress.com/2007/08/22/7-principles-of-an-eagle-dr-myles-monroe/

Get Up Giraffe
   Larson, C., Motivational Stories. *Learning to Get Back Up.*
   http://getmotivation.com/stories16.htm

How High Can You Jump?
   Ziglar, Z., (2000). *See You at The Top.* New Orleans, LA: Pelican Publishing.

Mule in the Well
   Author Unknown. http://msgboard.snopes.com/cgi-bin/ultimatebb.cgi?ubb=get_topic;f=82;t=000962;p=0

Rock
   Cavanaugh, B., *Obstacles? Deal with Them Now.*
   http://www.inspirationalstories.com/0/4.html

Sisu
   http://emiliaelisabethblog.wordpress.com/

Elephants Beeware
   King. L.D, Soltis J., Douglas-Hamilton, I., Savage, A., Vollrath F., McComb, K., *Bee Threat Elicits Alarm Call in African Elephants.* PLoS ONE, 2010; 5 (4): e10346 DOI: 10.1371/journal.pone.0010346

California Gold Rush
   Goal Setting for Success. http://www.goal-setting-for-success.com/california-gold-rush-story.html

Power of A Penny Doubled
   Michaels, S., *The Power of a Penny Doubled.*
   http://www.bellaonline.com/articles/art44195.asp

Two Frogs in the Milk

Author Unknown.

http://www.lifepositive.com/Mind/Teaching_Story/Two_frogs_in_the_milk102011.asp

Are You Building a Cathedral?

Author unknown. GPS for your organization. http://gpsoblog.com/tag/bricklayer

Sand and Stone

Author Unknown. http://www.story.net.in/2013/04/sand-and-stone.html

Two Ounces of Power

Britton, D. (Jan. 13, 2010). FCA Resources. *Two Ounces of Power.*
http://fcaresources.com/devotional/2010/01/13/two-ounces-power

The Problem May Be With Us

Author Unknown

A Leap of Encouragement

Author Unknown. http://www.crystal-reflections.com/stories/story_73.htm

The Power of Encouragement

Author Unknown

The Blind Men and the Elephant

Author Unknown. http://www.wordfocus.com/word-act-blindmen.html

Diamond in the Rough

National History Museum. http://www.nhm.ac.uk/print-version/?p=/nature-online/earth/rock-minerals/diamonds/diamond-formation/index.html

Pain

Powell, M., (Feb. 13, 2010). FCA Resources. *Pain.*
http://fcaresources.com/devotional/2011/02/09/pain

Relishing the Hard Button

FCA Resources. http://fcaresources.com

Opportunity

Cavanaugh, B. (2004). *The Sower's Seeds*. NJ: Mahwah. NY.Paulist Press.

Big Rocks

A Story of Priorities and a Jar.
http://www.sparkpeople.com/resource/motivation_articles.asp?id=264

How Do You Use Your Time?

Author Unknown

1000 Marbles

Davis, J. (2001). *1,000 Marbles*. Kansas City, MO: Andrews McMeel Publishing.

Run Towards the Roar

Morris, J., (August 16, 2007). *When you face trials, run toward the roar.* http://jimmorris.wordpress.com/2007/08/16/when-you-face-trials-run-toward-the-roar/

The Cafeteria of Life

Author Unknown. *Life is Like a Cafeteria.* http://www.goal-setting-for-success.com/life-is-like-a-cafeteria.html

Which Direction Do I Go?

Brooker, Will (2004). *Alice's Adventures: Lewis Carroll and Alice in Popular Culture.* London: Continuum.

The Rich Treasure

Author Unknown. *Aesop's Fable. The Farmer and His Sons.* http://www.first-school.ws/theme/fables/farmer-and-his-sons.htm

The Old Man and the Children

Author Unknown

Destiny

Author Unknown. http://www.spiritual-short-stories.com/spiritual-short-story-122-Destiny.html

Road Not Taken

Frost, Robert (1916). *"The Road Not Taken" from Mountain Interval.* New York, New York: Henry Holt and Company.

Little Fellow Follows Me

Claude Wisdom White. http://www.tomslighthouse.net/lighthse/foot129.htm

Water Bearer and the Pots

Author Unknown. http://www.clergyresources.net/med3.html

You Can Make a Difference

Author Unknown. http://andrew-ong.com/2008/02/06/the-starfish-story-you-can-make-a-difference/

Touchstone

Author Unknown. Daily Herald. http://www.heraldextra.com/news/local/the-secret-of-the-touchstone/article_5287cff5-5347-5b11-ba7b-b14d9cec31a9.html

Precious Present
> Johnson, S. (1984). *The Precious Present*. New York, NY: Knopf Doubleday.

Lifting Calf
> Author Unknown

Never Quit-Bamboo
> Author Unknown. http://mythologystories.wordpress.com/2013/01/17/never-give-up-inspirational/

Woodcutter
> Author Unknown. *The Woodcutter, a Fable.*
> http://jumproductions.com/articles/woodcutter.html

Stonecutter
> Author Unknown.

More Is Not Always Better
> Author Unknown. http://users.rider.edu/~suler/zenstory/more.html

Echo of the Mountain
> Author Unknown

Garbage Truck
> Pollay, D., (2010). *The Law of the Garbage Truck.* New York, NY: Sterling Publishing
> http://davidjpollay.typepad.com/david_j_pollay/lawofthegarbagetruck.html

Giant Slayer
> Fairchild. M., *David and Goliath Bible Story Summary.*
> http://christianity.about.com/od/biblestorysummaries/p/davidandgoliath.htm

Twenty Dollar Bill
> Author Unknown. http://home.comcast.net/~jptillman/stonecutter.html

Chicken and the Hen
> Author Unknown. *Chicken and the Eagle.*
> http://www.bankofideas.com.au/Stories/fables.html#Chicken

Positive Thoughts Lead to Positive Words
> Author Unknown. *Just Two Words.* http://users.rider.edu/~suler/zenstory/twowords.html

Seed
> Author Unknown

Attitude of Gratitude

United Nations World Census Reports. http://unstats.un.org/unsd/default.htm

Build Your Best House

Author Unknown. http://www.crystal-reflections.com/stories/story_74.htm

Are You a Team Goose?

Author Unknown. Everyday Mysteries.
http://www.loc.gov/rr/scitech/mysteries/geese.html

Blind Boy

Author Unknown. Moral Stories. http://academictips.org/blogs/the-blind-boy/

Growing Good Corn

Author Unknown. http://www.inspirationpeak.com/cgi-bin/stories.cgi?record=142

Rabbit and Turtle Race

The Rabbit and The Turtle Race. http://pinknetmoney.blogspot.com/2009/12/rabbit-and-turtle-race_10.html

The Ultimate Sacrifice

Canfield, J. and Hanson, M. (1993). *Chicken Soup for The Soul*. Deerfield Beach, FL: Health Communications, (pp.27-28).

Warwick the Mule

Simple Truths (Oct. 12, 2009). *Teamwork Lessons from Old Warwick*.
http://blog.simpletruths.com/old-warwick

About the Author

Dr. Mark Stanbrough is a professor in the Department of Health, Physical Education and Recreation at Emporia State University in Kansas. He teaches graduate and undergraduate exercise physiology and sports psychology classes and is the director of Coaching Education. The Coaching Education program at Emporia State is currently one of only ten universities in the United States to be accredited by the National Council for the Accreditation of Coaching Education. He was a co-founder of the online physical education graduate program, the first in the United States to go completely online. He received his Ph.D. in exercise physiology from the University of Oregon, and undergraduate and master's degrees from Emporia State in physical education. He has served as department chair and has served on the National Association for Sport and Physical Education National Sport Steering Committee and is a past member of the board of directors for the National Council for the Accreditation of Coaching Education.

Mark has over thirty years of coaching experience at the collegiate, high school, middle school and club level. Coach Stanbrough served eight years as the head men's and women's cross country/track and field coach at Emporia State (1984-1992) with the 1986 women's cross country team finishing second at the NAIA national meet. He has also coached at Emporia High School and Glasco High School in Kansas. He is a Level I and II USATF certified coach. Mark has served as the USATF Missouri Valley Association President and as the head referee at numerous national meets. He is a member of the Emporia State University Athletic Hall of Honor and the Health, Physical Education, Recreation Hall of Honor and has won numerous coach-of-the-year awards at the high school and collegiate levels.

www.ingramcontent.com/pod-product-compliance
Lightning Source LLC
Chambersburg PA
CBHW080937040426
42443CB00015B/3446